10 minute CRAFTS for SPRING

ANNALEES LIM

First published in 2013 by Wayland
Copyright © Wayland 2013

Wayland
338 Euston Road
London NW1 3BH

Wayland Australia
Hachette Children's Books
Level 17/207
Kent Street
Sydney, NSW 2000

Senior Editor: Julia Adams
Craft stylist: Annalees Lim
Designer: Emma Randall
Photographer: Simon Pask, N1 Studios

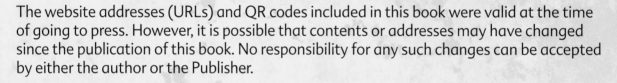

The website addresses (URLs) and QR codes included in this book were valid at the time of going to press. However, it is possible that contents or addresses may have changed since the publication of this book. No responsibility for any such changes can be accepted by either the author or the Publisher.

A CIP catalogue record for this book is available from the British Library.

ISBN 978 0 7502 7774 7

Printed in China

Wayland is a division of Hachette Children's Books, an Hachette UK company.

www.hachette.co.uk

Picture acknowledgements:
All step-by-step craft photography: Simon Pask, N1 Studios; images used throughout for creative graphics: Shutterstock

Contents

Spring

Spring is one of the seasons of the year. The months of spring are March, April and May. During spring, the days start getting longer and the weather gets warmer and often more sunny.

Spring is the time of year when things start to grow. Seeds germinate, and can grow into plants or small trees, called saplings. You can see the bare trees of winter turning green with lots of new leaves, too. Spring is also the time when many animals are born or hatch from eggs.

You can see lots of different weather in spring. It can be rainy, sunny or windy. Don't let that stop you from going outside to explore. Rubber boots are perfect for splashing about in spring showers. And don't forget to bring a waterproof jacket!

In this book you will find out about lots of natural materials you can collect while you're outside, and how to make great crafts out of them. But remember to be careful about what you collect. A lot is still growing and should not be picked. Anything that you do collect should be washed before you use it.

Fluffy sheep

If you get a chance to visit a farm or take a walk across some fields you might spot some newly born sheep. They are called lambs. Make your own countryside scene when you are at home by using some grass cuttings and balls of cotton wool.

You will need:
- A4 piece of thin blue card
- PVA glue and a paint brush
- cotton wool balls
- Black card
- Brightly coloured paper
- Grass cuttings
- Scissors
- Pencil

1

Paint some hills shapes onto a blue piece of card using some PVA glue.

Lots of baby animals are born in spring. Try using the grass to make a nest and the cotton wool balls to make some chirping birds that have just hatched from their eggs.

2

Sprinkle the grass cuttings over the PVA glue and shake off the excess.

3 Stick three cotton balls onto the grassy hills using PVA glue.

4 Make the heads and feet by cutting out the shapes from black card. Stick them to the cotton wool balls to create sheep.

5 Finish the picture by making some paper flowers and a shining sun. Stick them into place using your PVA glue.

The life of a seed

It may seem like new plants shoot up overnight, but they take some time to grow fully. Make this fun seed guide to remind yourself of all the steps a seed takes to turn into a blossoming flower.

1

Fold a piece of A4 paper in half, and in half again, lengthways. This will make four equal-sized rectangular boxes. Open out the paper.

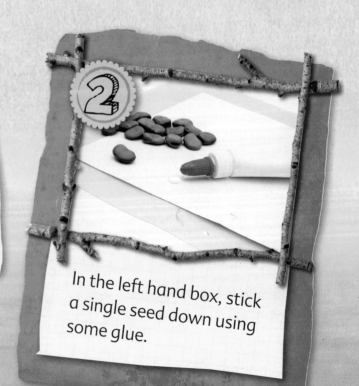

2

In the left hand box, stick a single seed down using some glue.

3 In the next box along, stick down another seed. Draw a small shoot onto green card and cut it out. Stick it above the seed.

4 Stick a seed in the next box along. Draw a larger shoot onto green card and cut it out. Draw a small bud on lighter green card. Stick both the shoot and the bud above the seed.

5 In the last box, stick down the final seed. Make a really long shoot out of green card. Draw petals on another card and stick everything above the seed to create a flower.

Leaf print flowers

Lots of sun and spring showers are the perfect combination to help plants grow. You may even find that they grow so big that they need to be trimmed back. Next time you are in the garden or a park, collect pruned leaves to do some printing.

1

Select some leaves that are different shapes; some short and round and some long and thin.

2

Apply paint onto a flat surface, such as a plate. Use a paint brush to spread the paint out in a thin layer.

3

Press a short, round leaf gently into the paint and print it onto a piece of paper. Leave lots of space around each print.

4

Using a long, thin leaf, press it gently into a different colour paint. Print six leaf shapes around one of the short round shapes.

5

Repeat this for each of the short, round shapes. You can use different colours for each flower to make your artwork as colourful as possible.

Daffodil paperweight

One of the earliest flowers to bloom in spring is the daffodil. Bring this pretty flower into your home by making a daffodil paperweight!

You will need:
- Egg box segment
- Pebble
- Craft glue
- Yellow felt
- Orange felt-tipped pen
- Scissors
- Scrap paper
- Pen

Use an orange felt-tipped pen to colour in the egg box segment. Leave to one side.

Do you know any other flowers that blossom early in spring?

Draw a petal shape onto a piece of paper. Cut this out to make a template.

3

Use the template to cut five yellow petals out of some felt.

4

Stick the five petals onto the pebble using craft glue.

5

Stick the egg box segment into the centre of the petals.

Bark rubbing

Forests and woods are full of exciting things, but you should leave most of them where you found them. One way to take a piece of the forest home with you is by making bark rubbings of some of the trees you pass.

1

Hold a piece of paper onto a tree trunk, and, using the side of a dark green crayon, rub it gently over the paper to reveal a rubbing of the tree beneath.

2

Repeat this three more times, using different colours: blue, brown and light green.

3

Stick the blue rubbings onto thin card using a glue stick.

4

Cut a trunk shape out of the brown rubbings and a tree canopy out of the light green rubbings. Stick them onto the blue rubbings.

5

Finish your picture by drawing the outline of a strip of grass onto the dark green rubbings. Cut it out and stick it onto the bottom of the paper.

Bouncing bunnies

If you are lucky, you may be able to see bunnies in spring. They are very shy, so you'll have to be quiet and patient to spot them. You can create your own bunnies, so that you can look at them whenever you like!

You will need:
- Different-sized leaves
- coloured card
- white paint
- Plate or paint pallet
- Scissors
- craft glue
- Googly eyes

1
Choose some leaves. Make sure some are small and round, some are big and round, and some are long and thin.

2
Paint a thin layer of white paint onto a flat surface such as a plate. Gently press the big round leaf into the paint and print it on the card.

3

Repeat with a smaller, round leaf, making sure the prints overlap.

4

Using the long, thin leaves, print two ears. You can print the bunny's feet and tail with your finger.

5

Stick a pair of googly eyes onto the big, round leaf print. Cut out when dry.

Watch this video to find out how to make a frame for your bunnies!

Twig hanging

When you look out of your window, you may be able to spot bright green leaves sprouting on lots of trees. Be inspired by the colours you can see to make a twig hanging that you can use to decorate your room.

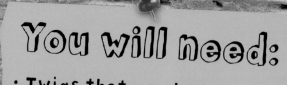

You will need:

- Twigs that you have gathered
- Brightly coloured wool

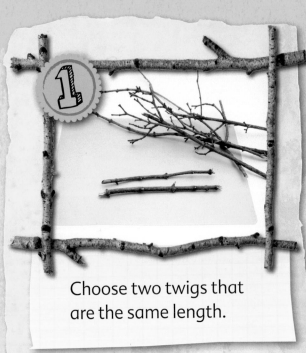

Choose two twigs that are the same length.

Using some wool, tie them together so that they form a cross.

Watch this video to find out how to make another kind of twig hanging!

3

Wind the wool once around each twig, repeating until you have covered a third of the sticks.

4

Attach a new colour of wool and repeat winding the wool around each twig. Use as many different colours as you like.

5

When you reach the ends of the twigs, tie the wool securely. Tie a loop in some wool and attach it to the end of one twig.

Potted flowers

These pretty spring flowers will stay in bloom all year! Ask an adult to help you find some flowers in your garden or the park. Place them in a piece of paper between two heavy objects to press them. Once they are dry, they are ready to use for this craft.

You will need:

- Press-dried flowers
- coloured card
- Scissors
- Three green lolly sticks
- Green craft foam
- craft glue and glue stick
- Small stones or gravel
- clay pot

1 Choose three dried flowers that you want to use. Stick each of them onto different coloured card.

2 Cut each of the flowers out and stick them on the end of a lolly stick.

Cut out some leaf shapes and stem shapes from the craft foam. Stick them onto the lolly sticks.

Fill a pot with some small stones.

Stick each of the lolly stick flowers into the pot.

Watch this video to find out how to decorate your pot!

Soil picture

Spring is the time when people sow seeds that grow into flowers, plants and even vegetables. They plant the seeds in the dark, rich soil. You can use some of this soil to make a fun bee picture!

1 Using a pen, draw some oval shapes onto a yellow piece of paper. Draw stripes onto each of the oval shapes. Add a sting to each of the shapes.

2 In each oval, paint a thin layer of PVA glue onto every other stripe.

3 Sprinkle some soil over the wet PVA glue and shake off the excess.

4 Cut out some paper wings and stick them onto each bee.

5 Stick a googly eye onto each bee.

Always wash your hands after touching soil!

Glossary

bark the rough outer layer of a tree's trunk and branches

germinate when a seed germinates, it begins to develop, growing a stem, leaves and roots

hatch when an animal breaks out of an egg

prune to trim a tree or bush

sapling a young tree

sow to plant seeds in the ground

template a shape you can draw around again and again to make the same shape

Index

10 minute CRAFTS

Titles in the series:

AUTUMN
978 0 7502 7772 3

Pine cone squirrel
Apple hedgehog prints
Dried leaf bonfire
Field mouse
Spider web
Mini owls
Scarecrow
Book worm
Conker creatures

SUMMER
978 0 7502 7771 6

Crawling crabs
Butterfly pegs
Seascape in a bottle
Sandcastles
Flower prints
Mini kites
Sunflower pot
Rafts
Starfish

SPRING
978 0 7502 7774 7

Fluffy sheep
Life of a seed
Leaf print flowers
Daffodil paperweight
Bark rubbing
Bouncing bunnies
Twig hanging
Potted flowers
Soil picture

WINTER
978 0 7502 7773 0

Mini pine forest
Bird bingo
Twirling twig hanging
Bird feeder
Sticks and stones
Scented hanging
Ice mobile
Potato print snowman
Penguin skittles